*E*veryone, at one time or another, goes through stages in their relationships. How else can couples build and grow, understand and forgive? It's all a part of being in love.

If we remember to keep that in mind, we can find a way to work through anything. We just have to believe in each other and believe in our love.

— T. L. Nash

Love Isn't Always Easy

*A Blue Mountain Arts® collection
about working through the
difficult times... together*

Blue Mountain Press™

SPS Studios, Inc., Boulder, Colorado

Library of Congress Catalog Card Number: 2001003488
ISBN: 0-88396-601-8

ACKNOWLEDGMENTS appear on page 64.

Certain trademarks are used under license.

Manufactured in China
First Printing: August 2001

✪ This book is printed on recycled paper.
This book is printed on fine quality, laid embossed, 80 lb. paper. This paper has been specially produced to be acid free (neutral pH) and contains no groundwood or unbleached pulp. It conforms with all the requirements of the American National Standards Institute, Inc., so as to ensure that this book will last and be enjoyed by future generations.

Library of Congress Cataloging-in-Publication Data

Love isn't always easy : a Blue Mountain Arts collection.
    p. cm.
ISBN 0-88396-601-8
1. Love poetry, American. I. SPS Studios (Firm)
PS595.L6 L588 2001
811.008'03543—dc21

                                                                2001003488
                                                                CIP

SPS Studios, Inc.
P.O. Box 4549, Boulder, Colorado 80306

Contents

Love Isn't Always Easy

Love doesn't mean that you will never feel pain or that you'll live a life free from care. It doesn't mean that you will never be hurt or that your life will be perfect, with every moment consumed by happiness.

Love does mean that you will always have a companion, someone to help you through the difficult times and rejoice with you in your times of celebration. It means that each argument is followed by a time of forgiveness, and each time of sorrow is far outweighed by all the tender moments spent in each other's arms.

Love is the miracle that can take two lives and mold them into one, take two souls and bind them for life, take two hearts and fill them with enough passion and tenderness to last a lifetime.

Love is a blessing that will lead you down life's most beautiful path.

— Michele Weber

I'll Put the Past Behind Us
If You Will

Whatever problems we've had, either spoken or felt, whatever feelings have been hurt for whatever reason, whether it's been because of a lack of communication or too much communication, we cannot change what's come between us.

I think sometimes communication can actually make things worse because it may not be possible to explain all the reasons we act the way we do. We may not be capable of understanding each other's problems, no matter how hard we try, or be able to process every comment, piece of advice, and attitude into the truth as it was intended. We just may not be strong enough to deal with certain things because of all that's going on in our lives at the moment.

I sense a wall going up between us. I liked life better without it, and I hope you did, too. To say "I'm sorry" is an understatement... I'm sorry if I've been insensitive to your situation. I'm sorry if I failed to understand something that you thought I should. I'm sorry for whatever's wrong and for all the reasons it turned out this way. I'm sorry if you're having a hard time dealing with something in your life and for anything I did or didn't do that has caused our relationship to be less than it was.

I know some things are hard to talk about, but I just wanted you to know that I'd like to patch up whatever's wrong. I'd like us to get along. I miss that comfortable feeling we had with each other. Life is so short; I don't want there to be tension or bad feelings between us. I want the best for you. I want you to be happy. I'll put the past behind us if you will, so we can get on with tomorrow.

— *Donna Fargo*

I Love You,
Even Though Things Are Not
Always Perfect Between Us

No one is perfect
therefore no
relationship can be perfect
Often by seeing
the dry brown petals
in a rose
you appreciate more
the vivid red petals
that are so beautiful

At the core of our relationship
there is a very deep respect and love
for one another
so as we continue
to grow and change as individuals
our relationship will continue
to grow stronger
and become more beautiful
I love and appreciate you
so much

— Susan Polis Schutz

Thank You for Being Patient with My Difficult Moods

I appreciate so much
how you're able to put up with my moods.
I try so hard, but sometimes my moods
get the best of me;
I get sad, and sometimes I get angry
because I think you should
understand and comfort me.
Yet I know you can't understand
when I shut you out;
you can't comfort me if I refuse to let you.
Sometimes, I feel like crying
for no reason at all.
I realize that's hard to understand,
but it's my way of letting go
of all the anger, hurt,
and frustration that's inside me.

I let things around me
influence the way I act;
I let the past in,
and my feelings from then
get tangled up in my feelings now.
I guess this has to happen sometimes,
and I know it hurts you.
But it's a part of growing,
   learning, and living.
Thank you for understanding
when I'm quiet,
and for being patient when
you're frustrated with me,
because without you
my life would be incomplete.
Always remember that I love you.

— Kelly S. Murray

In our busy lives, we often forget that there is more along the way than just bills to pay, phone calls to return, and errands to run. There are people in our lives who need to be hugged, who need to be loved. There are people in our lives who need their accomplishments to be noticed and praised. We need to remember how fragile hearts can be, how quickly a soul can grow weary, how fast a spirit can break.

Forgive me for forgetting that a heart is like a garden that needs to be tended to and nourished with what only another heart can give — love and appreciation, devotion and honesty.

— Tracia Gloudemans

My Favorite Fantasy?
A Little More Time
for You and Me

*I have a special hope that someday
our relationship will find a way to be
filled with more time.
Just for the two of us.
I don't think anything would
make me happier than that.*

*And I love to think of how wonderful
it would be...*

*I have a favorite fantasy that takes us to
a place where we have all the time in the
world; a place where we have quality and
quantity time. That would be paradise to me.*

It would be heavenly to find a way in our everyday lives to slow the world down and take away some of the pressures — moments when the demands of making a living take too much away from making a life. My fantasy gives us more time to smile and relax. To show how much we care. To share our love. To say what's in our hearts and on our minds.

I'd love to have more time for moments like this... where we can reflect a little on our goals and our being together, and where I can have all the time I need... to tell you that I'm going to be in love with you forever.

— Susan Channel

You Are So Important to Me

*W*e both have things in our lives
that cause stress.
Even though we know when this happens
and we try to keep it from
influencing our relationship,
the extra burdens affect
our moods and actions
and how we get along.
I think we need to realize this about ourselves
and work a little harder
to prevent it from happening.
If each of us can have
more patience and understanding,
and be more aware of what is being said
and how it affects our feelings,
maybe we can keep these outside feelings
from having a damaging effect on us.

We'll probably need to compromise more
and give each other some needed space.
Maybe it'll take an extra smile or hug.
All I know is that I'm willing
to do whatever it takes to keep us together
and feeling as happy and secure
as we both know we can be —
because you are so important to me.

— Barbara Cage

I Promise, Honey...

I'll Try Harder

The next time I don't take the time to think before I speak, I'll try to look ahead to where it will lead us. I'll try to stop myself in mid-cycle before an argument has the time or a reason to be born. When something touches the rough edges of my soul and I take things too personally, I'll try harder to slow down and not just react.

I'll try harder not to jump so fast the next time you don't act the way I think you should. When I'm expecting one thing and you do another, sometimes your words and actions surprise me and catch me off guard. That's not an excuse; it's just a circumstance that I'm trying to understand so I can change.

I'll try to be a better listener and to be more thoughtful in my conversation with you. I'll try to adjust my attitude to take more responsibility for my own reactions and to live in a spirit of cooperation with you. I'll try to be a little quieter and not talk so much. I'll try to treat you with the same consideration I'd treat a friend, because with friends, I'm sure I wouldn't jump as fast and act the way I do at times with you.

I know I'm too sensitive sometimes, so I know how it feels when words hurt, and I just want to apologize for any hurting things I may have said to you. I guess relationships are never perfect, but I want ours to be. I love you so much, and I don't want to be the cause of any of our conflicts. Your own words and actions should be yours to judge, and I should take responsibility for mine, so I just want you to know that I'll try harder.

— *Donna Fargo*

Even Arguing Is Sometimes a Part of Being in Love

I wish we could have problem-free days every day, and spend all our time laughing and enjoying each other. It sounds wonderful, but it's not realistic.

We are going to have those days when we fight and make ourselves crazy, when words are exchanged and feelings get hurt. And there will also be days when we are as close as two people can be, sharing and creating memories that are very important to us.

People argue and disagree, just like you and I. But that doesn't mean there's anything unusual about us. Everyone, at one time or another, goes through stages in their relationships. How else can couples build and grow, understand and forgive? It's all a part of being in love.

If we remember to keep that in mind, we can find a way to work through anything. We just have to believe in each other and believe in our love.

— T. L. Nash

Every once in a while
I start feeling a little lost,
especially when I start thinking back
  to where we've been
and when I start wondering
  where we're going.

And every now and then...

I need some things from you
  that I don't always get...
I'd like for us to just
talk a little more
and touch a little more;
there are lots of times when
I could use a reassuring hug
  and the smile that I love to see...
just an occasional sign
that you're still happy with me.

I'm not asking for much...
  just enough to know
    from time to time
    that I make a difference.
For just knowing that
makes all the difference
  in the world to me.

— A. Rogers

Sometimes when you look at me,
I wonder if you see
all the love that shines in my eyes
only for you.

Sometimes I wonder if you see
in my smile
the special touch of happiness
that comes from loving you.
When you look into my eyes,
I feel you reaching deep within my soul,
and I wonder if you see
all the beautiful light in me
that comes from your love.
I wonder if you see
my arms reaching out
to hold you with tenderness and warmth.
I wonder if you see
the fullness of my heart
and the precious feelings
our love brings.

Sometimes I want to tell you
to look with your heart,
and you'll see that
everything I have to give
is only for you, for always.

— Linda Sackett-Morrison

What Does "I'm Sorry" Really Mean?

What does "I'm sorry" really mean? "I'm sorry" can be an apology for acting in a way that was very insensitive. And even though feelings weren't meant to be hurt by those actions or words, it's understandable how they can be. In all kinds of ways.

There are times when the stress of the day simply carries over into other parts of life. Sometimes, when one's frustration level — with all that needs to be done — fills up to the brink, it's pretty easy to say something stupid without even thinking of the harm it will do. It's no excuse, but it happens sometimes.

And I'm sorry when anything like that happens between us. Please... I hope you'll try to understand everything that "I'm sorry" implies, because it would break my heart to think I made you sad and chased away some of the smiles in your eyes.

— Douglas Pagels

Expressing Hurt Feelings May Be Hard, but It Is Important

Sometimes it may not seem
that I love you
Sometimes it may not seem
that I even like you
It is at these times
that you really need to
understand me more than ever
because it is at these times
that I love you more than ever
but my feelings have been hurt
Even though I try not to
I know that I am acting cold
   and indifferent

It is at these times that I find it so hard
to express my feelings
Often what you have done to
hurt my feelings is so small
but when you love someone
like I love you
small things become big things
and the first thing I think about
is that you do not love me
Please be patient with me
I am trying to be more honest
with my feelings
and I am trying not to be so sensitive
but in the meantime
I think you should be very confident that
at all times
in every way possible
I love you

— Susan Polis Schutz

*S*ometimes even in the best relationships,
people let situations and emotions take control.
Things are said and done
    that make it difficult
    and uncomfortable.
However, if the people involved
    can look at the problem
with a clear perspective,
    they can usually figure out
how to fix it, compromise,
    or let it go.

— Barbara Cage

*L*ove is more like a flower than a tree:
    the wrong things can hurt it so easily,
    but the right things can make it more
        beautiful and more fragrant than
        anything else your life has ever known.

— Barin Taylor

Appreciating the
Differences Between Us

For us to have a relationship
of lasting value,
we must appreciate
the differences between us.
We must respect those differences,
because they are the foundation
of what makes us unique.

It is the differences I see in you
that first attracted me to you.
There is an excitement in your eyes
that has captured my heart.
There is an independence within you
that I strive to attain.
You speak your mind and heart
when I feel so caged up inside.

You have dreams and aspirations,
and nothing will get in your way.
You show all sides of your character —
both the passionate and the difficult.
Despite all that you have endured in life,
you have a unique quality
of love and gentleness.
I appreciate you
probably more than you know.
I have come to love the differences
between us,
and I respect you for
the beautiful person
that you are.

— Sherrie L. Householder

In order to have
*   a successful relationship*
you need to put out of your mind
any lessons learned
*   from previous relationships*
because if you carry
*   a sensitivity or fear with you*
you won't be acting freely
and you won't let yourself
*   be really known*

In order to have
*   a successful relationship*
it is essential that both people
be completely open and honest

— Susan Polis Schutz

The Keys to Love

The key to love is understanding...
the ability to comprehend
not only the spoken word,
but those unspoken gestures —
the little things that say
so much by themselves.

The key to love is forgiveness...
the capacity to accept each other's faults
and pardon mistakes,
without forgetting —
but by remembering
what you learn from them.

The key to love is trust...
though dark doubts
lie in hollowed thoughts,
it must shine on brightly
with reassuring radiance
that suppresses fear with faith.

The key to love is sharing...
facing your good fortunes,
as well as the bad, together —
both conquering problems and
forever searching for ways
to intensify your happiness.

The key to love is giving...
  without thought of return,
  but with the hope of just
  a simple smile,
  and by giving in, but never up.

The key to love is respect...
  realizing that you are
  two separate people
  with different ideas —
  that you don't belong to each other,
  but that you belong with each other
  and share a mutual bond.

The key to love is inside us all...
  it takes time and patience
  to unlock all the ingredients
  that will take you to its threshold;
  it is a continual learning process
  that demands a lot of work...
  but the rewards are more than
  worth the effort...
And you
  are the key
    to me.

— Robert M. Millay

I Wish I Knew
the Perfect Way
to Love You

Because my love isn't perfect, I place expectations on you and then feel disappointed when you don't always meet them. I make you into someone greater than myself, and then I wonder why you tumble down into ordinariness. I can't believe that the greatness I project on you could ever be within me.

Because my love isn't perfect, I am frightened sometimes that you will leave me. I'm frightened of being alone. Sometimes I hold you so tightly that I suffocate your spirit, and then I wonder why you are unhappy. I forget that love needs space in which to grow.

You deserve to be loved in a perfect way, and I hope you can forgive me for any time my love is less than perfect.

— Stephanie June Sorrell

I Only Want to Love You

Why do I put you
through such misery
when I love you
so much
Why do I act so moody
with you
when I love you
so much
I want you to understand that
my moods are
not aimed at you
They are usually due
to something that happened
during the day
but when I see you
I seem to withdraw into
a quiet madness

I am not taking out my frustrations on you
I am just letting my frustrations out
in front of you
because I feel
so comfortable and real with you
In fact
I am able to solve and understand
my problems in this way
I am very sorry
for causing you confusion and
for making you upset
Thank you for trying
to understand these moods
and for letting me feel
so natural with you
You are so important to me
I never want to hurt you
I only want to love you

— Susan Polis Schutz

It's funny sometimes how
even though we love
and trust one another,
we can still leave so many words
unsaid between us,
so many wishes unspoken.
There are times, I'm sure,
when we've both wanted to be
listened to, to be held —
but our inner words and
    our outer signals
were too quiet to be
noticed by the other...

If we were able to be
as close and as communicative
as I would like us to be,
hardly a word would go unspoken
    that needed to be heard;
hardly a touch would go unheeded
    that needed to be felt;
hardly a day would go by
    without us
        falling more in love.

— *Laine Parsons*

*There is no difficulty that enough love
will not conquer; No disease that enough love
will not heal; No door that enough love
will not open; No gulf that enough love
will not bridge; No wall that enough love
will not throw down; No sin that enough love
will not redeem...*

*It makes no difference how deeply seated
may be the trouble;
How hopeless the outlook;
How muddled the tangle;
How great the mistake.
A sufficient realization of love will dissolve
it all... If only you could love enough,
you would be the happiest and most powerful
being in the world...*

— Emmet Fox

In everyone's life,
there are problems to solve.
Even in the strongest relationship,
there are differences to overcome.
It is easy to give up when confronted
with difficulties —
to fool yourself into believing that
perfection can be found somewhere else.
But true happiness and a lasting
relationship are found
when you look inside yourself for
solutions to the problems.
Instead of blaming the other person and
walking away when things get tough,
look for compromise and forgiveness.
Caring is not a matter of convenience.
It is a commitment of one soul to another.
And if each gives generously of themselves,
then both lives are enriched.
The problems will come and go,
just like the changing seasons.
But unselfish love is constant
and everlasting.

— Susan Staszewski

Bad Things Can Happen to Good Relationships ...but I Want Us to Always Work Things Out

*I don't want us to go in
separate directions.
 I want us to stay together.
I don't ever want to lose you.
 Of all the people the whole
  world over, you are the
   one I treasure.
I don't want to make you sad.
 I only want to see you happy.
I don't want us to argue.
 I want us to always find
  ways to work things out.
I don't always know what words to say.
When times are hard, the right words
are the ones that seem so far away.
 I just want you to understand...
I don't ever want us to drift apart.
 I want us to keep our love
  alive, and I want you to realize
  that you will always be the
  inspiration behind the happiness
  that smiles in my heart.*

— L. N. Mallory

I Come to You in Peace and Forgiveness

Let's just start over, wipe the slate clean. Let's stop holding on to what went wrong and forgive each other and go on. We're only hurting ourselves. Let's stop letting disappointment and blame keep us bound. We can't change the past, but we can change tomorrow.

All we have is our own lives. I have no right to tell you what to do with yours any more than you have a right to tell me what to do with mine. I'm sorry for what I did or didn't do that didn't please you, but I'm not perfect, and I can't undo any of it now, no matter who was right or wrong. We may never understand it all, but what's done is done. It's over. Let's turn the page right now and move on. I will if you will.

We each make decisions according to our perceptions of the circumstances at the time. Sometimes we're right. Sometimes we're not. And we can't know now how things would have been if we'd acted differently. Since we are the only ones who can make things right, I need you to do this with me. We shouldn't be estranged from each other.

I forgive you. Will you forgive me? I come to you in peace. Accept me and all my imperfections, and I'll accept you. We can't change the past, but we can start over and change tomorrow. Let's do it.

— *Donna Fargo*

Don't Be Afraid to Love

Don't be afraid
to love someone
totally and completely
Love is the most fulfilling
and beautiful feeling in the world
Don't be afraid that you will
get hurt
or that the other person
won't love you
There is a risk in
everything you do
and the rewards
are never so great
as what love can bring
So let yourself get involved
completely and honestly
and enjoy the possibility
that what happens
might be the only real
source of happiness

— Susan Polis Schutz

"One Thing Will
Never Change"

*Life is so unpredictable. Changes always
come along... in big ways and small steps,
sometimes giving us a little nudge and
other times turning our whole world
upside down. So many changes; some
subtle and almost unnoticeable, some
drastic and more difficult to deal with.*

*But throughout all of life's changing and
rearranging, I'm so glad that
there is one wonderful thing
that will never change...*

In the passing of life's moments, I know that yesterday is already gone and that tomorrow will soon be here. The one thing I will take with me in all the days that lie ahead... is the one thing that has seen me through so many times in the past.

It's something that will never change.

You are such a steady, strong, and beautiful part of my life. You never cease to amaze me with the constancy of your giving, the unselfishness of your heart, and the reassurance of your smile.

And I thought it would be nice to let you know that my special feelings for you are going to last

forever and ever and ever.

— Marta Best

*You Don't Ever Have
to Worry About...*

My Love for You

*With so much going on in your life — all
the directions you feel you're being pulled in —
I wanted you to know that I'm always in your
corner. I love you, and you can depend on me
whenever you need me. Maybe that sounds too
simple, but it's the truth. You mean everything
to me, and I never want you to believe otherwise.*

*I want you to always feel safe and secure and,
most of all, loved by me. That's what I'm here
for. I want to be the person you come home to
every day and tell your worries to. I want to
be able to encourage your heart or soothe your
troubled mind. When it comes to your happiness,
I want to be the one who takes care of you.*

*There is enough going on in your life now
without your having to worry about whether
I love you enough to stick by you. So in case
you were wondering... the answer is and always
will be... absolutely!*

— *T. L. Nash*

With Love,
We Can Overcome
Any Differences

Sometimes, we allow our differences to come between us. In attempting to defend our individual beliefs and prove that one of us is "right" and the other "wrong," we argue and push each other away. We feel the separation and distance created by anger and fear. But this isn't what I want for us.

Let's stop being angry and fearful because we have different views on some things; let's start expressing love and appreciation for one another.

Let's be open enough to respect each other's right to have our own beliefs, ideas, and values. Let's appreciate and focus on what we have in common: our love.

If we focus on the goal of being "right," then we will be divided by our differences. But if we focus on the goal of expressing and sharing love, we will overcome the distance and stand together, united by love.

I want there to be peace and love between us, not distance, because I value our relationship and I truly do love you.

— Donna Newman

I Will Love You...

As long as I can dream,
as long as I can think,
as long as I have a memory...
   I will love you.

As long as I have eyes to see
and ears to hear
and lips to speak...
   I will love you.

As long as I have a heart to feel,
a soul stirring within me,
an imagination to hold you...
   I will love you.

As long as there is time,
as long as there is love,
as long as there is you,
as long as I have a breath
   to speak your name...
   I will love you,
because I love
   you more
   than anything in
   all the world.

— *Daniel Haughian*

No Matter What
I Say or Do,
I Love You

*I know we have our unhappy moments... when
things aren't going great or we hurt each other's
feelings or we say things in the heat of an argument
or we do things we wish we hadn't. But after the
storm is over, after we try to see each other's side,
after we calm down and put things in proper
perspective, after we apologize and ask each other's
forgiveness... we realize that we're just not perfect
so all our rough edges are not smoothed out yet and
we don't show our love perfectly... and then we
forgive each other and go on.*

*As much as I try to change my ways, become more
mature in my thinking, learn patience, slow down
enough to listen and be objective and not take
things so personally, I mess up sometimes and say
or do something that tries to ruin the whole picture
of our love. I just want you to know that I am
always so sorry for that.*

I also hope you will always remember that those hasty words and careless acts are not indicative of my true feelings. They are just fleeting, momentary displeasures. They are unprocessed emotions, my immaturity speaking, my unguarded reactions. They are not the whole picture, but rather just a little blot on the corner of the canvas of our relationship. The truth is... I love you all the time, even when things aren't perfect. I say things that hurt sometimes because I'm hurt.

I sometimes do things without thinking of your feelings, and at times I just do things without thinking of the consequences of my own actions. Please understand that I never mean to hurt you. I think sometimes part of the problem is that men and women are different; we react differently to situations and see things at times only from our own perspective. Please forgive me when I'm not sensitive to your needs and feelings.

Through it all, I hope that you can trust in the fact that I love you, no matter what I say or how I act. I will continue to work on trying to show my love to you in a more loving way, so that there is no doubt in your heart and mind that I love you. I don't want you to think that I'm copping out and excusing my behavior when my actions seem insensitive and unloving. I'm not perfect, and I just want you to know that I love you and I will always love you.

— Donna Fargo

One of the most valuable lessons
we can learn from life is this:
Try as we might,
    we will never have all the answers.
We can wonder for the rest of our days
    whether we are doing the right thing...
        continuing in the best relationship,
        and following the best paths toward tomorrow,
but no one is ever going to
    answer those questions for us.

We both may have wonderings of what to do
and curiosities of what's to come.
Time will help us with the results,
    but more than any one thing,
        it's up to us — and to the love
            we have for each other —
        to go in the right direction.

You and I sometimes wonder
    about where we're headed
and whether our love will last a lifetime through.
We may not know the answer, but
I'll tell you the one thing I do know:
        There's no one I'd rather try to spend
            forever with... than you.

— Collin McCarty

ACKNOWLEDGMENTS

The following is a partial list of authors whom the publisher especially wishes to thank for permission to reprint their works.

PrimaDonna Entertainment Corp. for "I'll Put the Past Behind Us If You Will," "No Matter What I Say or Do, I Love You," "I Promise, Honey...," and "I Come to You in Peace and Forgiveness" by Donna Fargo. Copyright © 1998, 2001 by PrimaDonna Entertainment Corp. All rights reserved.

The following works have previously appeared in Blue Mountain Arts® publications:

"The Keys to Love" by Robert M. Millay. Copyright © 1981 by Robert M. Millay. "In everyone's life, there are problems..." by Susan Staszewski. Copyright © 1982 by Susan Staszewski. "I Will Love You..." by Daniel Haughian. Copyright © 1984 by Daniel Haughian. All rights reserved.

"It's funny sometimes how even though we love..." by Laine Parsons, "One of the most valuable lessons..." by Collin McCarty, "Every once in a while..." by A. Rogers, "Thank You for Being Patient with My Difficult Moods" by Kelly S. Murray, "Love is more like a flower..." by Barin Taylor, "Sometimes when you look at me..." by Linda Sackett-Morrison, "Love Isn't Always Easy" by Michele Weber, "With Love, We Can Overcome Any Differences" by Donna Newman, "My Favorite Fantasy?" by Susan Channel, "Sometimes even in the best relationships..." by Barbara Cage, "Appreciating the Differences Between Us" by Sherrie L. Householder, "I Wish I Knew the Perfect Way to Love You" by Stephanie June Sorrell, "'One Thing Will Never Change'" by Marta Best, "Even Arguing Is Sometimes a Part of Being in Love" and "You Don't Ever Have to Worry About..." by T. L. Nash, "In our busy lives, we often forget..." by Tracia Gloudemans, "You Are So Important to Me" by Barbara Cage, "What Does 'I'm Sorry' Really Mean?" by Douglas Pagels, and "Bad Things Can Happen to Good Relationships" by L. N. Mallory. Copyright © 1983, 1986, 1987, 1989, 1990, 1992, 1997, 1998, 1999, 2001 by SPS Studios, Inc. All rights reserved.

A careful effort has been made to trace the ownership of poems used in this anthology in order to obtain permission to reprint copyrighted materials and give proper credit to the copyright owners. If any error or omission has occurred, it is completely inadvertent, and we would like to make corrections in future editions provided that written notification is made to the publisher:

SPS STUDIOS, INC., P.O. Box 4549, Boulder, Colorado 80306.